Catorce Enero 29 de 1908

Real de Catorce, Mexico ————

The Incredible City

By Lucy H. Wallace

AMIGO ENTERPRISES
Publishers

P. O. Box 427   Mission, Texas 78572

This book is dedicated to the friendship of the people of the United States of America and of the Republic of Mexico as exemplified by their presidents, the late *John Fitzgerald Kennedy* and *Adolfo Lopez Mateos.*

ACKNOWLEDGMENTS

The author wishes to acknowledge valuable assistance from the following who made this book possible:

To Charles F. McClelland, author of the idea for the book; Francisco Hermosillo and Padre Albino E. Enriguez of Real de Catorce; Mrs. Helen Jones, and Perez Quijano, of Matehuala; Roberto Cuadro of the San Luis Potosi Mining Association and Maria de Bueron Barcena of the San Luis Potosi State Tourism Department; Mrs. Pedro Corsi, San Luis Potosi; R. C. Clardy of Mission, Texas; Marcos Coronado and Marcos Guerrero of Estacion Catorce; Mrs. Maria Luisa de Quijano of San Luis Potosi; and many others.

Lucy H. Wallace

8

This is Catorce

Six hundred residents of a time-stands-still town high on a Mexican mountain stand guard and wait for the return of the adventurous spirits who peopled the town in its hey-day — a time when fortunes were made by the turn of a burro's hoof and lost by the slap of a card on a gambler's table.

Once the home of 25,000 residents whose pride and ambitions claimed the nation's attention, Real de Catorce in the mountainous state of San Luis Potosi even today beckons those who like to remember the glamorous Yesterdays and dream of fabulous Tomorrows.

Its very name spells mystery and intrigue. The "Catorce" (which means 14 in Spanish) was inspired by the stories of fourteen bandits who hid out in the Sierra Mountains to waylay gold-bearing cart trains. The "Real" (Royal) was added when rich ores were discovered and by decree a percentage of the mines' production was claimed by the King of Spain.

Today, Real de Catorce can show the casual visitor stories of romance, violence, beauty, tragedy, art, ugliness, history of a colorful past — the hope of a new future. It promises adventures unlimited for those whose special interest might be minerals or gem rocks, cacti or antiques, to coin collectors, camera fans, history buffs or architects.

History does not make clear the fate of the fourteen *Bandidos* (highwaymen) who first were lured to the mountain hide-out by its inaccessibility. Today, Real de Catorce is still not easily accessible and perhaps that is the principal reason that it represents an oasis unchanged in the changing world that describes Mexico of today.

But riches other than silver and gold are promised the traveler who takes the time and trouble to discover them today.

Superlatives abound here. The altitude of 9,043 feet makes it the highest city in Mexico, possibly on the North American continent.

No other town — certainly no other in the New World — is approached through a tunnel. Built first for a narrow gauge railroad to take out the silver ores which latter-day engineers were unlocking from the mountain store-house, the tunnel is now Real de Catorce's best link with the outside world.

Today's traveler to this Yesterday Town arrives at the tunnel over twisting mountain trails from Matehuala, "parent" city of Real de Catorce. (Prospectors from Matehuala first discovered the rich veins of silver ore in 1773 and later used smelters at Matehuala to process the ores.) Trails carved by burdened burros are now followed by pick-up trucks or four-wheel drive jeeps to take modern adventurers to the mountain retreat.

As if the tunnel is not surprise enough, another unexpected wonder lies within. Literally carved into the passage is a recess which forms a tiny chapel where candles burn perpetually. Here fresh flowers are placed daily on the exquisite little altar in memory of miners who have lost their lives within the core of the mountain — and to guard those whose days carry a continuing threat of repeating tragedy.

An architectural jewel, the chapel asks a few moments of worship from the casual traveler as well as the miner whose daily passages echo by its portal.

Bright sunlight leads one dramatically out of the tunnel for the first view of the incredible city spread on the curving mountain side. Unlike the one-street ghost town of America's Old West with its unpainted shacks which foretold its early doom, Catorce is a living monument to its builders. Here, the upper echelon Spaniards who followed the glint of gold brought along their love of the luxurious life.

Here distinctive architecture bears the stamp of Colonial Spain bringing a pictorial quality flooded with charm. Thick-walled mansions of stone are laid on three and four levels of the mountain top, graceful fountains center plazas rimmed with the old homes decorated with iron gargoyles and balconies of wrought iron "lace."

Cobble stones which pave the streets of the 200-year old town are laid in patterns which hint of primitive engineering while they testify that its builders meant for their town to live after them.

Catorce's air of permanence makes it a sister city to other historic mining towns of Mexico, Taxco, San Miguel de Allende, Zacatecas. But these have been protected by Government edict as "monument" towns which insures that they will always retain their ancient appearance. Even if new buildings are added, these have a built-in patina to match the authentic old ones.

No such ruling has protected Real de Catorce but the weathered look is here as if frozen by Father Time. Because its buildings are of stone, maintenance of those occupied is nil. However, enough of the old homes have been deserted to warrant the terminology of "ghost town" — even while its present day citizens talk of bright tomorrows when a road will be built and the almost deserted mines are back in full production.

Who can say what lurks in the ghostly shadows? What promise lies in the mines that hold the key to a better life tomorrow?

Through This Tunnel

Chapel is carved back into mountain from tunnel
La Capilla está embutida en la montaña detras del túnel

Suddenly, a winding road through another ghost town, La Luz, ends with an entrance to a tunnel. This is The Ogarrio, finished in 1901 by the mine companies who laid narrow gauge rails and installed mule-drawn carts to take the ores eastward for rail connections. Passenger carts were brought in and the service, such as it was, depended on mule-power here also. Later, an electric "tranvia" was installed to give the passengers a more modern accommodation.

But the mines closed about 1910 — because of the Revolution — and flooding followed during the years of inoperation. The rail line was abandoned soon afterwards. In the 1930s, the rails were taken up to be sold for scrap and the tunnel came into use for the general public.

Today, an occasional truck or jeep passes through, carrying supplies to Real de Catorce. Still more rarely come tourists in jeeps or pick-up trucks sturdy enough to travel the rugged trail.

Owners of Dolores Mine built the chapel within the tunnel, calling it Nuestra Senora de los Dolores (Our Lady of Sorrows). It was dedicated to the men who lost their lives in mining accidents.

Today's miners who work the mines on a small scale consider the shrine as a part of their protection. They and their families pause before the altar daily, bringing candles to light or fresh flowers to place before the painting of "the Lady."

One enters through an arched portal — there is no door to be closed. The elaborate stone pillars and frescoes indicate the work of a dedicated artist-designer. The chapel is about eight feet wide and twelve feet deep.

The tunnel is so narrow that no vehicles can pass each other except at one turn-out. However there is so little traffic that this rarely becomes a problem.

Miners place candles, flowers on altar daily
Los mineros colocan velas y flores en el altar de diario

14

Sunlight beckons as the traveler nears tunnel exit overlooking fantastic city

Los rayos del sol alumbran al veiajro cerca de la salida del túnel a la vista de la fantástica ciudad

Tunnel was built to bring out silver ore

El túnel se construyó para acarrear el mineral de plata

Miners pose with sacks of ore (about 1904)

Los mineros posan sobre los costales de minerales (más o menos en 1904)

Electric tramcar, 1902, was first modern transportation

La primera transportación moderna fué en tranvia eléctrica en 1902.

Passengers rode behind mule over rail line through tunnel

Los pasajeros viajaban en carreta tirada por una mula sobre rieles

CATORCE S.L.P.
Desfile Escolar.
-Centenario 1,910.

Track, long since removed, was narrow gauge (Celebration here marks centennial of school system)

La vía férrea mucho antes removida era estrecha medida. (Aquí se celebraba el Centenario del sistéma escolar.)

17

Chapter
2

SALÓN COMEDOR

EN LA VISITA QUE HIZO EL C. PRESIDENTE DE LA REPUBLICA GRAL., DE DIVISION
DON PORFIRIO DIAZ.   AÑO DE 1.896.   CATORCE. S.L.P.

SOCAVON DE SANTA ANA.
EN LA VISITA QUE HIZO EL C. PRESIDENTE DE LA REPUBLICA GRAL., DE DIVISION
DON PORFIRIO DIAZ. AÑO DE 1.896. CATORCE. S.L.P.

Mine entrance decorated for visit of Presidente Diaz

Socavón de la Mina Santa Ana está adornado con motivo de la visita de C. Pdte.
de la República Porfirio Díaz

CABALGATA HISTORICA - CONJUNTO.

EN LA VISITA QUE HIZO EL C. PRESIDENTE DE LA REPUBLICA GRAL., DE DIVISION DON PORFIRIO DIAZ. AÑO DE 1.896. CATORCE. S.L.P.

Citizens costumed as Spanish royalty lead parade for Diaz

La cabalgata Histórica en honor del C. Presidente de la República General Porfirio Díaz fué precedida por ciudadanos vestidos de Regalía Española

GRUPO DE LA INDEPENDENCIA.

EN LA VISITA QUE HIZO. EL C. PRESIDENTE DE LA REPUBLICA GRAL., DE DIVISION DON PORFIRIO DIAZ. AÑO DE 1.896. CATORCE. S.L.P.

Father Hidalgo, patriots remembered in parade

El grupo de la Independencia incluye al Padre Hidalgo y sus compatriotas

Early records in the archives of the principal church, La Parroquia, tell of the beginning of Real de Catorce as a separate village. It is believed that the first rich ore strike was in 1773. The church records begin with the first death in 1777, recorded by the first priest, Father Pedro de la Vega. These records date events which preceded the building of Parroquia when the principal church was La Capilla, still standing and in use. It is located in the Panteon (cemetery) and is used principally for funeral services now.

Father de la Vega recorded the death of Margarita, eight-month old daughter of Juan Martinez and Juana Petra Carells Martinez, in 1777. Baptismal rites were recorded July 1, 1779 at La Capilla for Jose Manuel Indio, the first in Father de la Vega's records. The first wedding ceremony was noted the same year. Here, Juan Ramon de la Picon, a Spaniard, took as his bride Maria Blasa, a Mestiza.

Most carefully kept of all records are those of the mines which have been the subject of several books and statistical reports filed prior to 1800 or soon afterwards. These emphasize the mineral treasures which gave Real de Catorce its reason for being. These have been thoroughly authenticated and serve to verify the dates for other events that make the town's history so fascinating.

Famed Baron Humboldt was one of the first and most famous writers to take note of Real de Catorce. In his book, "Political Essay on New Spain," published in 1804, Baron Humboldt counted the Catorce mines as third in the quantity of production of all New Spain. In one of his comments, the noted minerologist-nobleman said "The mines of Catorce rank second or third place among the mines of New Spain, if they are classified according to the silver they produce.

"Those of Catorce and the veins of Chota in Peru are the most important in the history of Spanish America in the past two centuries. To mine here, there is no need of costly machinery to drain the water."

Highlights of Catorce's colorful past have also been preserved in the municipal records on file at the City Hall. There are volumes and volumes of minutes, some transcribed as early as 1796. Still earlier, mines of the Catorce area were registered at Charcas, headquarters for all mining in that section of Mexico during that period. Here, the first mining claim in what was to become Real de Catore was registered in 1773.

From that date on to today, the mines hold the key to the vein that mingles a glorious past, a static present and a hopeful future. As more mines were discovered and worked, the torrents of silver flooding forth made silver "kings" of fantastic wealth. (By 1779 there were more than 100 different mines — at one time, there were more than 300 claims filed in one year.)

Thus the mining economy was the core of both the power and the culture of the city that began to grow around the mines.

The mines brought the luxury-loving Spaniards whose way of life almost two hundred years ago is reflected in the beautiful old homes made of stone, untouched by time. They brought the peons that swelled the population to the thousands, come to work the mines for a bare living that is hinted at in the crumbling adobe houses on the back streets.

Culture came in the persons of the owners, the engineers and superintendents whose families demanded the luxuries they had left behind. Soon the city boasted an opera house, theaters and a social life which flowed through salons, theaters and gardens patterned after the rich old haciendas of Spain or the elegant town houses of Mexico City's socially elite.

Was it fourteen bandits or fourteen brave soldiers who gave the intriguing name to this mountain city? One early historian has revealed that the town's original name was "Senora Nuestra Concepcion de Guadalupe de los Alamos." However, the residents never fully accepted this lengthy approach to saying "my hometown." Possibly the length of the official name was one reason they glee-fully insisted that "Real de Catorce" was much better.

Another student of the town's history has suggested that it is small wonder that the legend's beginning is forever lost — in those days, it was often difficult to tell whether a soldier was a bandit — or a soldier.

From the beginning, residents of Real de Catorce have known that theirs was no ordinary city. They came to expect that many notables would be their guests. They knew that the Fiestas they staged would be more exciting, more colorful than those celebrated in a provincial village. The religious pilgrimage today that brings thousands to their city each October 4 is unequalled anywhere else in Mexico. Pageants and parades which note national holidays here are somehow more glorious than those staged in much larger cities.

The richness of the mines helped to build these superlatives and set the pattern for other facets of life in Catorce. The bonanzas were wilder, the gamblers who tossed away their earnings so nonchalantly lost in greater amounts.

Even the bandits who came in 1910 to disrupt the mine work found incomparable loot. Where else did marauders ride away from the homes they had plundered wearing silk opera hats and Homburgs straight from Europe's fashion centers?

Leonardo Covarrubias, native of Real de Catorce, at 84 remembers seeing as a young man those bandits parade through the streets so decked in the finery they had found in the homes of mine owners or engineers. For saddle blankets, the bandits (Revolutionists) had folded the beautiful damask draperies snatched from the windows of the homes abandoned when the owners fled ahead of the bandits.

The most exciting three days in the city's history marked the visit of its most famous and most distinguished visitor, General-Presidente Porfirio Diaz. The time was 1896 and the occasion was the dedication of new modern machinery in one of the mines.

MOCTEZUMA Y SU SEQUITO.

EN LA VISITA QUE HIZO EL C. PRESIDENTE DE LA REPUBLICA GRAL., DE DIVISION
DON PORFIRIO DIAZ. AÑO DE 1.896. CATORCE. S.L.P.

Citizens portray Emperor Montezuma, Court in parade

Los ciudadanos representan al Emperador Moctezuma y su séquito

A wonderful parade was organized in the Presidente's honor with the towns-people portraying the Catholic Kings of Spain, Don Fernando and Dona Isabel, Christopher Columbus, Emperor Montezuma II of Mexico, Hernan Cortez, the conqueror, and his Captains. Others were costumed as Emperor Maximilian and his beautiful Empress Carlota, then the beloved Patriot-President Benito Juarez and his ministers.

Catorce was at the peak of its glory and this was apparent wherever one looked, the older residents of today recall. At every intersection of the narrow streets along the parade route, arches of flowers were placed. At night on the flat roofs of all the houses and the church, "luminarios" burned, fed by oil wicks in earthen pots. Great fires burned on the peaks of the mountains that rim the city.

President Diaz was entertained at a banquet in the home of the owner of Santa Ana mine at La Luz. He sat at the head of the long table in the ornately-decorated room. The guests (all men) were resplendent in bright uniforms or formal dinner dress.

Today, such an occasion could be copied only in the great capitals of the world.

Municipal band, circa 1900, has cultural role
La Banda Municipal representa la parte cultural

1937 fiesta crowd in Main Plaza
En la Plaza Príncipal se ve el gentío para las Fiestas Patrias del 1937

A town surrounded by bare hills
Un pueblo rodeado de cerros llanos

Old smelter (right) is now converted to apartments . . . rent is six pesos per month (48 cents, U.S.)

La antigua fundidora (a la derecha) se ha convertido en viviendas las cuáles se rentan a razón de seis pesos mensuales.

Protective cross is dedicated
La Cruz Protectora es dedicada

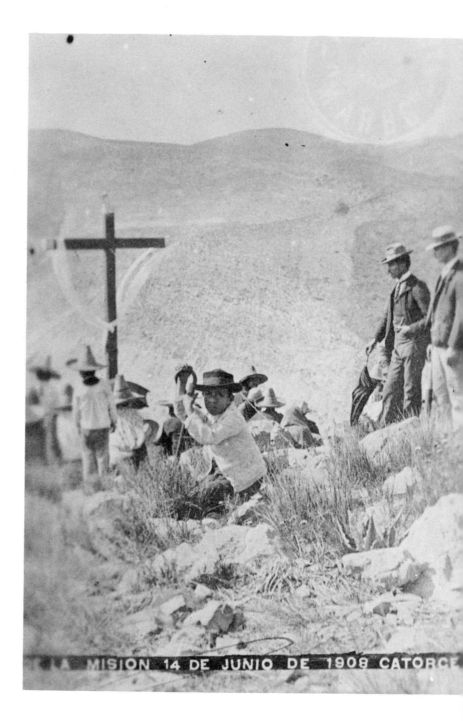

LA MISION 14 DE JUNIO DE 1908 CATORCE

Past splendors of their ancestors' way of life reflect the daily patterns of Catorce's population today. Genteel and soft-spoken, Catorce's people of today center their lives around their religion. This devotion is evident to the visitor on his first glimpse of the city. On the peaks of the mountains that rim the city, its people have erected tall crosses on craggy rocks that appear almost totally inaccessible.

"We think of these crosses as a protection for our city and all who live in it," Francisco Hermosillo, one of the leading citizens, explains. Senor Hermosillo, the City Treasurer, is the only resident who speaks English alhough a few young people are studying the language.

Of the 100 present-day families, many live in the old stone houses built by their ancestors. Some of the fine old homes were closed when the owners moved away. But caretakers are on duty, hinting of the hopes that the owners will return.

An "Old World" charm is evident in the manners of the people, in their attitude toward strangers and each other. Visitors are greeted with courtly politeness, in spite of the limited language communication in most instances. Little boys, arriving at the church for catechism or on an errand, greet the priest by kissing his hand.

Crime is almost non-existent — at the Palacio Municipal (City Hall), officials cannot remember when the jail was last used.

In the memory of today's residents, only one edifice has been built. This is the new parochial school and playground, dream-come-true of Padre Albino E. Enriquez. He called it "Parque Juan XXIII" for the late beloved Pope John.

On the streets of Real de Catorce today, one sees very few men simply because most of them work away from home while they continue to hope that the mines will re-open. Or some other economy, such as tourist interest, could bring a new era for their community, they tell each other.

Some of the men work in the small mines operated over the mountain near Station Catorce, west of Real de Catorce and on the railroad. Others take the limited agricultural products to the railroad town to sell.

School classes dismiss while teacher buys vegetables
Las clases se suspenden mientras la maestra hace sus compras.

Trunk of one variety of cactus is peeled, sliced and eaten
El tronco de cierto nopal lo pelan, lo rebanan y lo comen

Old men, young boys offer antique hardware for sale
Ancianos y muchachas ponen en venta antigua ferretería

From the maguey (cactus variety sometimes called the "century plant"), the men extract agua-miel, a popular and vitamin-packed drink when fresh drawn. Others harvest and sell the heavy crop of "tuna," fruit of the most prolific cactus in the area.

There are a few orchards of peach, quince and apple trees, a few grape vineyards that yield a money crop. Another cactus yields fiber to make ixtle and this is readily marketed in Matehuala.

Goats abound in great herds, seeming to thrive on the sparse vegetation. These, too, are a factor in the economy as they provide both meat and mohair wool.

The greatest hope of most of the residents is that a road will be built to Cedral, 25 miles away, to connect Real de Catorce — after two centuries — with the outside world.

"This could be another Taxco," the City Councilmen say as they speak of the advantages of climate and local color.

"With tourists coming, we could convert some of these old mansions into hotels for them," the spokesmen add.

As an example of their hopes for the city's future, the town fathers have been accumulating a fund to begin work on the road. Their idea is that by showing the Federal Government their willingness to help themselves, they can enlist support to finish the road.

Because Real de Catorce was founded by the Spanish in a spot that was unoccupied before the mines were opened, there is no "Indian" background in today's population. Unlike most Mexican towns, Catorce has no Indian crafts, costumes or folkways — no market day to attract visitors such as tourists or residents from near-by towns.

There are no curio stores, no soft drink machines, no street vendors offering food or souvenirs to sell.

Goats ask little food, water
Las cabras póco comen y beben

ARCO ALEGORICO "EL PROGRESO" EN LA PLAZA
HIDALGO. CATORCE. S.L.P.

Early merchant's imagination, pride in his hometown reflects civic enterprise
En esta foto se refleja el espíritu emprendedor de los primeros comerciantes

Palacio Municipal (City Hall) is hub of community
El Palacio Municipal es el centro de la comunidad

Transportation — 1773 or 1965 — unchanged

La transportación no ha cambiado desde 1773.

Occasional visitor is money-buyer, seeking old coins

El visitante ocasional llega comprando antiguas monedas

Women, children carry most of the water

Mujeres y niños acarrean casí toda el agua

National holidays inspire fiesta for whole city
Los días de Fiesta Nacional inspiran festividad para todo el pueblo

38

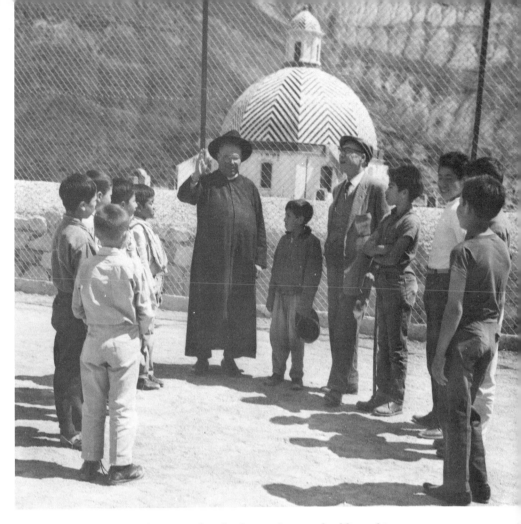

Padre built new playground, school — only new building this century

El párroco construyó la escuela nueva con su patio de recreo (el único edificio nuevo hecho en este siglo)

Caves dug out of mountainside, a family's home

Estas cuevas, cavadas en la montaña, sirven de viviendas

Rocky front wall encloses cave-home
La pared hecha de piedras encierra la casa cueva

Mountain-man has broad shoulders, over-sized lungs
El hombre de la montaña es de anchos hombros y fuertes pulmones

Fiesta, early 1900's, indicates population peak in Catorce's history

En la historia de Catorce esta fiesta a principios de 1900 indica su populación en la cumbre

Rarity of snowfall is celebrated by youngsters in downtown plaza

Un caso raro de nevada es celebrado por los niños en la plaza principal

St. Francis –
Whose Shoes Wore Thin

St. Francis statue holds place of honor

La estátua de San Francisco mantiene su lugar de honor (una página de cuatro fotografiás todas representan milagros)

44

A distinction which has made Real de Catorce famous all over Mexico and in many other lands is its image of St. Francis of Assisi, held in great veneration by all of the population and all those who once lived there. Now set in a place of honor in the principal church, La Parroquia de la Purisima Concepcion, the image is the subject of many legends. Most important, it is the object which brings four or five thousand pilgrims to Catorce each October on the feast day of the saint.

Most favored of all the legends is the one which tells of St. Francis appearing before a *campesino* (worker on a ranch) in the area, promising him great wealth.

A favorite story with all gives the saint (or his image) a very human trait. This dates back to the time when the image was placed in La Capilla, the smaller chapel that is older than La Parroquia and the original church for the community. With the completion of La Parroquia, most of the parish activity began to be centered there.

But St. Francis had been left behind in the old chapel. The parishioners continued to go to the old chapel to pray before their favorite, however. Soon, so the stories go, they began to notice that his shoes were becoming thin and worn, progressively so as time went on. They reasoned that he was wandering the streets at night, unhappy in his loneliness.

At last it was decided in 1850 (some seventy years after his "unhappiness" started) to move the statue to La Parroquia. After that, the parishioners gleefully report, his shoes never wore thin again.

All year long, the pilgrims come, bringing silver "milagros," the small silver "miracle" medals to pin on his robes. These are reproductions of parts of the body, animals, persons or even inanimate articles helped in some way after prayers to St. Francis. The custom is popular throughout Mexico and not limited to St. Francis in other churches.

The person who has been helped by the particular prayers offered (in this case) to St. Francis buys a silver or gold "milagro" which matches the part of the body which has been helped, the crop of corn which thrived, the house repaired. Then the tiny medals are taken to the church and hung on the saint's robes or placed nearby as a testimonial of gratitude.

SAN FRANCISCO DE ASIS; MILAGROSA IMAGEN QUE SE VENERA
EN LA PARROQUIA DE LA PURISIMA CONCEPCION. CATORCE. S.L.P.

Pilgrims come from many lands to bring Milagros

Los peregrinos vienen de muchas partes a ofrecer los milagros los cuáles los colocan en su manto

"Miracle Medals" (Milagros) represent prayers of thousands

Estas medallas milagrosas representan la fe de miles de personas.

Since the St. Francis of Real de Catorce is so old and has so many beloved legends told about him, his robes carry a vast testimonial to the faith he has invoked.

"We have a feeling that our St. Francis is more powerful and more sympathetic to our prayers than other images of the same saint," the townfolk of Catorce will tell you.

Each October 4, on the feast day of St. Francis, thousands of the devout come to ask for good health, riches, safe return of loved ones, etc., or to offer thanks for such favors received in answer to prayer.

So many come that for two or three days before and after October 4, the population is multiplied many times over. Some remain overnight and must sleep in the streets.

A few years ago, the saint's day brought tragedy. A truck stalled in Ogarrio tunnel, holding back dozens of vehicles in the cavalcade behind it. Before the traffic could start moving again, carbon monoxide fumes asphyxiated a child and endangered the lives of others.

Many of the pilgrims who come each year are former residents or their descendants. In addition to the milagros, some bring gifts of great value.

A short time after the end of World War II, three men who had served in the U. S. Navy came to see St. Francis, bringing a large model of a sailing ship which they had made and then covered with gold.

La Parroquia de la Purisima Concepcion, the present home of St. Francis, was built in 1780. It was financed by the old Spanish custom of permitting miners to take each day out of the mine as large a piece of ore as one could carry in his hand. This the miners gave to the parish priest as an offering and the proceeds were used to construct the beautiful church. Its cost at that time was said to be $1,800,000. Additions since then have added to its value.

Like the rest of the city, the church is built on several levels with portals on two streets. The court-yard is encircled by iron fences called "barandales," copies of similar decorations used in Old Spain.

Near-by is one of the city's principal fountains where many of the residents obtain their household water supplies.

Statues of Apostles atop church cut pattern against billowing clouds

Las imágenes de los apóstoles sobre la iglesia son cómo moldes reflegados ante oleadas nuves del cielo

50

Church is nerve center of the town, its daily life (Eroded hills in background)

La iglesia es la fortaleza central del pueblo su vida diaria (ha gastado los cerros al fondo del cuadro)

Chapter
5

Houses are stacked in tiers against mine-scarred mountains

Las casas en filas de unas sobre otras se ven contra montañas cicatrizadas por las minerías

Old stone houses reflect Spanish influence

Antiguas casas de piedra reflejan la influencia Española

CUARTEL

*Balconies, stone carvings are tribute to pride, ambitions of
luxury-loving Spanish aristocrats*

*Los balcones, y esculturas en piedra son tributos al orgullo y ambición de la
aristocracia Española amante del lujo*

Weathered doors are held together by hand-wrought nails

Puertas ya curtidas por el tiempo se detienen con clavas hechos a mano

55

Ancient "blue rocks" form intricate pattern to pave streets

Antigua pizarra formando enredadas formas es el pavimento de las calles

Town is nested in Sierra Catorce Mountains, shaded by their summits

El pueblo se encuentra anidado y sombreado por la cumbre de la montaña Sierra Catorce.

Each street leads eyes toward mountains
Cada una de las calles da frente a los montañas

Plaza is heartbeat of community life, faced by church, city hall, and centered by fountain

La plaza es el centro de la comunidad, tiene su fuente y está enfrente la iglesia y al lado el Palacio Municipal

59

Old smelter — each small window was opening for a furnace

Antiguo fundidor — cada ventanilla era abertura para un horno

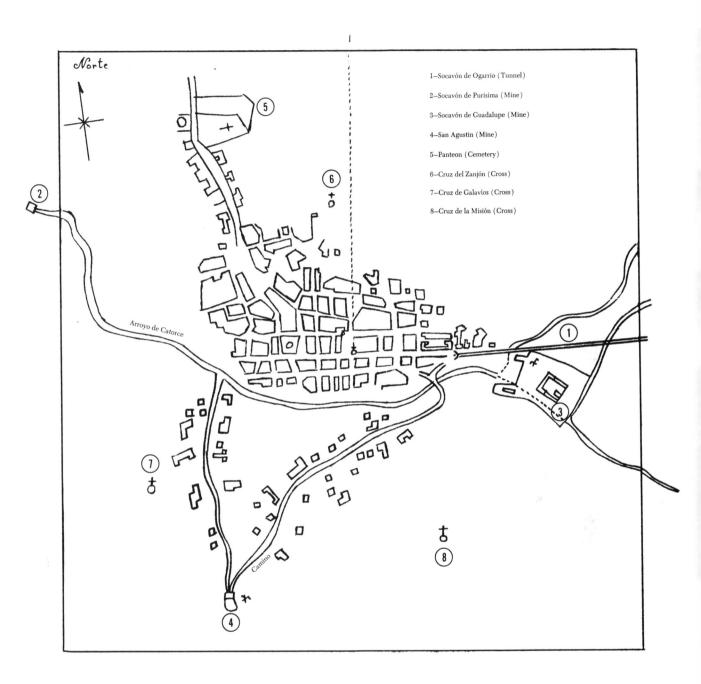

Norte

1—Socavón de Ogarrio (Tunnel)

2—Socavón de Purisima (Mine)

3—Socavón de Guadalupe (Mine)

4—San Agustin (Mine)

5—Panteon (Cemetery)

6—Cruz del Zanjón (Cross)

7—Cruz de Galavíos (Cross)

8—Cruz de la Misión (Cross)

Arroyo de Catorce

Camino

Casa Moneda (House of Money) was mint, home of elegance
"Casa Moneda" era la fábrica, casa de elegancia

Some of the most intriguing facets of Real de Catorce's history concern its Casa de Moneda, House of Money. Silver coins minted there during its brief operation (1863-69) are considered the second most rare — and most valuable — of all Mexico's. Copper coins minted there were once declared contraband by the Mexican Government and those found circulating them were subject to fines.

Currently, coin dealers specializing in the large silver pesos (eight reales) struck at Casa Moneda with the C-e mark list one in good condition as worth $250.00, U. S.

In the archives of Catorce's Palacio Municipal, historians may sift out an interesting story of how Casa de Moneda came to be and the problems this involved. Visitors today are impressed with the beauty of the house which was built to serve as a home for the owner as well as the mint which he operated under contract with the Government to process the coins.

One of the most imposing and substantial structures in the city, Casa de Moneda is still owned by descendants of the original owner, Santos de la Maza. It is also called Casa Maza. Three stories high, Casa Maza sits on the corner opposite the main entrance of La Parroquia Church. There are entrances to the old "House of Money" from both streets but on two different levels.

The great carved stone facade faces the church and is centered by a huge door of thick wood, set with heavy, hand-wrought hardware. Balconies rimmed with wrought-iron railings curve around windows of the two upper floors facing the other street. These are decorated with iron gargoyles and more carved stone trimming.

Within the house, the caretaker (and only occupant) shows visitors the rooms decorated with mural wallpaper and the inner courts which speak of past elegance. One court has balustrades made of ceramic around wooden dowels. The spacious rooms have thick walls and high ceilings and all open on the inner courts, typical of Old Spain.

Don Santos de la Maza was the author of the idea for a mint to be established in Catorce. Legends tell that one of the reasons the Don's proposal was endorsed by the City Council was that the bandits were waylaying the pack "trains" taking ore and silver bars out to Matehuala.

A great deal of strategy was involved before Don Santos saw his dream come true. The site which he picked was actually a large part of the main plaza of the town. Before the transaction could be legal, permission had to come from both the Governor of the State of San Luis Potosi and from the President of the Republic, Benito Juarez.

Beautiful facade was part of bargain
La hermosa fachada fué parte del contrato

65

Part of the transaction stipulated that Don Santos de la Maza would build the Casa Moneda with a beautiful facade. This agreement was met and the entrance is there today for all to enjoy its beauty.

In some of the correspondence connected with setting up the local mint, the City Council sent a letter to President Juarez stressing several good reasons for asking that he grant permission for the mint to be established; Catorce had received no favors from the Federal Government, they said, nor had it ever asked any before this; yet Catorce had indeed benefitted all of Mexico by sending out vast amounts of silver; and, they said, the proposed mint would help the prosperity of Matehuala and the entire state of San Luis Potosi as well as Catorce.

In due time, the requests bore fruit and the famous coins with the C-e mark are the result. Today, one of the ground-floor rooms of Casa Moneda still has the original scales used to weigh the silver, several molds in which the silver bars were shaped and a vault enclosed with heavy iron bars where the silver was stored.

Descendants of Don Santos tell a ghost story about the old house. Sometimes at night, the story goes, one may hear the clink of money being counted. Doubters in the family have been known to rush towards the sounds — to find nothing. Others firmly believe that the old Don has returned to count the coins once pressed in his mint.

The name of His Majesty, Emperor Maximilian, Archduke of Austria and Emperor of Mexico (for a short time), entered in Catorce's history in 1866. On May 26 of that year, the City Council sent their ruler a letter which cited the benefits of the local mint and petitioned him that its operations not be closed. They pointed out that the mint had attracted commerce and industry to their city; that it boasted the best of equipment for making the coins and that the operation had attracted influential and distinguished persons to the city as permanent residents. Its closing would be a great loss in many respects, they concluded.

But in spite of all the pleas and the negotiations, the mint was closed in November, 1869. (In the meantime, the Emperor had come to the end of his short reign over Mexico and Juarez was again the head of the Republic.)

The four-volume work on the coins of the Mexican Republic, written by Dr. Pradeau, states that the mint was opened May 18, 1863, and continued (except for several brief suspensions) until November 28, 1869. The silver coins were struck only in denominations of 8, 4 and 2 reales. All carried the one date of 1863.

In Spanish Colonial times there was a provisional mint in Real de Catorce in 1811. This mint issued only 8-real coins, all dated 1811. These were, of course, very limited in number and are extremely rare today.

Copper coins which bear the C-e mark are also much sought after by collectors. Some bear the date of 1822 and are believed to have been issued for distribution within the area only. This was a custom at one time in the early years of the Republic when each state or mining area was granted the privilege of minting copper coins only.

Worn copper coins bear C-e mark, dated 1822
Moneda de cobre muy gastada tiene la marca C-e hecha de 1822.

Iron gargoyles, balconies are decorative

Gárgolas de fierro, los balcones son decoraciones

One part of "Money House" has three floors
Una parte de la "Casa Moneda" tiene tres pisos

Mold was used to shape silver bars; vault in background

Este molde se usaba para formar los barras de plata; Al fondo se ve la bodega

Coins were issued during a six-year period. (These are eight- and four-real pieces—very rare).

Reverse side of coins show 1863 date.

Medal, date unknown, is also collector's item.

Las monedas fueron puestas en circulación por períodos de seis años. (En la fotografía se ven monedas de ocho y cuatro reales que son muy raras). El revés de las monedas muestran el año 1863. No se sabe la fecha de la medalla. También ésta es artículo para colectores.

The Panteon (Cemetery)

Chapter 7

Main entrance leads to Guadalupe Church, oldest in Catorce

La entrada principal conduce a la iglesia de Nuestra Señora de Guadalupe, la más antigua en Catorce

Funeral processions file through this gate — there are no vehicles
Pallbearers carry corpse on their shoulders, mourners walk behind

El cortejo fúnebre pasa por ésta puerta . . . no acompañan coches, los que van
con el cadaver lo llevan en los hombres. Los dolientes le siguen a pié.

Burial customs in Real de Catorce are much like those in other Mexican villages. Church bells ring to announce a death and the news is also spread rapidly by relatives and neighbors.

Friends bring gifts of food, candles and flowers to the home of the dead. There is no undertaker but loving hands prepare the body for burial. The coffin is usually made hastily by the town carpenter. The dead are not embalmed and burials take place within 24 hours of the death. (This is true all over Mexico, in the cities as well as the villages.)

Children are often dressed for burial in the costumes of a favorite saint. For instance, the bodies of little boys may be dressed like St. Joseph or St. Francis, the little girls like the Virgin Mary.

There is no hearse. When the time arrives for the funeral, friends acting as pallbearers literally carry the corpse on their shoulders up the steep street that leads to the Panteon.

When time allows, the body lies in state a few hours before the funeral in the Muerte Room — Room of the Dead — in the cemetery. This tiny chapel is centered with a stone bier large enough for the coffin to be placed in the center and for candles to be placed around it.

Earliest dates noted on grave stones are in the early 1800s. However, church records list the first death in 1777. Within Guadalupe Church (on the grounds of the cemetery), several members of prominent families have been buried beneath the stone floor. Their gravestones lie flush with the floor.

This church pre-dates the main church which is in the center of the city (La Parroquia).

Dedicated to Our Lady of Guadalupe, the patron saint of Mexico, the older church has a painting of the saint above the altar. On the walls are several beautiful paintings and the dome is especially well proportioned.

Gates to the Panteon are kept locked but the guides who take visitors into Catorce can secure the key from the City Hall or the priest at La Parroquia Church.

"Muerte" Room — Room of the Dead — is tiny chapel near church
Here deceased lies in state before funeral

El cuarto de la Muerte es una capillita cerca de la iglesia. Aquí se expone el cuerpo del finado.

Bridge at approach to cemetery is called "Puente de Jesus" (Bridge of Jesus)

El puente que está al acercarse al panteón se llama "Puente de Jesus"

nte de Jesus.
orce, S.L.P.

Earlier photograph (about 1900) of Bridge of Jesus shows better condition; small shrine is in center niche

En la fotografía anterior (cómo el 900) del "Puente de Jesus" se ve en mejor estado; una capillita está en el nicho central.

Church, cemetery are on mountain slope

La Iglesia y el panteón están situados en la ladera de la montaña

Grave stones behind Panteon wall show dates of early 1800;
church records show earliest death was in 1777

En las piedras de las sepulturas detras de la pared del panteón se encuentran
fechas hásta del 1800; los archivos de la iglesia tiene una de la primeras muertes
registrada el 1777.

Photo of 1930 era shows walls, roofs of buildings now fallen; cemetery dominates center

Esta foto de 1930 muestra una área de paredes y techos de edificios ahora destruídos. El cementerio está situado en el centro

Mountains cut by steep trails rim cemetery
(Right, center from mountain above it)

Las montañas cortadas por derechas veredas bordan el panteón (a la derecha
y al centro de la montaña sobre él)

Cross beside mountain road marks spot where man was killed;
relatives bring flowers, candles on death anniversary

La cruz a un lado del camino señala el sitio donde se mató un hombre; los deudos
ponen flores y velas en cada aniversario de su muerte.

SOCAVON DE PURISIMA CATORCE S L P

Guadalupita Mine is one ear-marked for re-opening
La Mina de Guadalupita es una de las que se cree se volverá a abrir.

Many fascinating myths are connected with the discoveries of rich silver lodes in the Catorce Mountains. Woodcutters found shiny veins of ore in the roots of scrubby trees. A musician became lost returning from a dance and camped out overnight. The next morning, he found molten metal where he had built his warming fire. Another discovered the precious metal while looking for his lost burro.

Ventura Ruiz, going down in local history as "El Negrito," found his own Heartbreak Hill in the mountains of Catorce. A Spanish soldier stationed at a mountain outpost, Ruiz was returning alone from Matehuala when he became lost. Deep in the mountains, he stumbled on a rich and abundant silver vein — and was rich overnight.

Ill-equipped for such sudden wealth, Ruiz received little benefits from it. He was illiterate and could not even count well enough to be sure that he was paid correctly for the sale of his rich ores. At the gambling table, his luck soon ran out. Within two years of his 1773 discovery, he was glad to sell his title for enough to buy a small ranch. There he died in poverty and obscurity. The mine he sold became San Agustin, one of the richest of all in the area.

Legends such as these add color to the area history but the true wealth of the region is shown in records of the City of Catorce, the San Luis Potosi Mining Association and the State of San Luis Potosi.

These records confirm the date of 1773 of San Agustin Mine's discovery, sometimes referring to it as "Veta de Milagros (Vein of Miracles) of San Agustin. Other explorations followed quickly, including some considered even today to have great potential wealth.

All of the early production came from near the surface. Later when some of the richest bonanzas were worked, the operators still did not have the advantage of modern methods and equipment. This is one of the principal reasons that owners of the mines today plan to re-open them, taking advantage of modern equipment to unlock the stores of riches already proven. Most of the students of the area's mining history agree that the mines were never worked to full scale under the old and rather primitive methods.

Another lure for the owners today is the price of silver, much higher than ever before. Also, recent legislation by the Government of Mexico is more favorable to the industry.

At one time, more than 300 claims for new discoveries were filed in one year, San Luis Potosi Mining Association records show.

Baron Alejandro de Humboldt, whose "Political Essay on New Spain" (1804) is considered the earliest and most authentic survey of modern economics in Mexico, was most enthusiastic in his report of the mines of Catorce. He rated them third in importance in Mexico and reported on the superior grade of silver in the ores. His report said that 400,000 marks in silver had been taken from the Catorce mines by 1796.

Baron Humboldt counted Catorce with Guanajuato and Zacatecas in saying that the three areas together were producing (at the time of his report) more than one-half of Mexico's annual production of 2.5 million marks in silver. This was at the peak period of the Colonial enterprise when Silver was King and the mines of Mexico doubled the world's silver supply.

In another part of his report, the learned baron made the statement that the importance and future expectations of the Catorce mines was greater because "there is no need for costly machinery to drain the water."

(Today, more than 150 years later, this point no longer holds true for the need to drain the mines is the first stumbling block faced by the owners who plan to restore the mines.)

Another early report set the figure of 4 million pesos for the production totals between 1778 and 1810.

La Purisima Mine was one mentioned in the Humboldt report. In one week in 1795, the production here was $60,000 — a figure which would be considerably higher at today's exchange rates.

Over the years, Purisima produced several bonanzas. Baron Humboldt's report showed the 1796 production to be $1,200,000 while the operating costs were only $80,000.

BONANAZA DE LA MINA SOCAVON DE "DOLORES TROMPETA"
CATORCE, S. L. P. JUNIO DEL AÑO DE 1902

In his book, "Las Minas de Mexico" (1905), J. R. Southworth tells of La Purisima's discovery in 1780 by woodcutters. They sold their discovery for $300. Under the new owners, La Purisima was soon developed and during the period of 1787 to 1803, the average annual production was $2 million.

In 1803, the figure hit $3.2 million but soon afterwards, the ore began to run down in value. The ores here were "colorado" (red), earthy carbonates of lead, horn silver and red ochre. With depth, there were also pyritous and copper ores, Southworth reported.

Production of all the mines in the Catorce District in 1905 totaled almost $4 million, Southworth's records show. A constant production of high grade ore made this possible.

Another mine which sold originally for a small sum, then was developed to reach astoundingly high production was the Padre Flores Mine. Many mining engineers consider this mine the richest of all. Some go still further and predict that its days of glory are not ended. When and if it should be re-opened, another rich era will unfold, they believe.

Historians recount that Padre Flores, a priest in charge at Real de Catorce, purchased the discovery for $700 in 1774 and named it "La Bolsa de Dios" — God's Money Bag. He dedicated its earnings to his faith and accomplished many things for the Catholic Church in the area with profits from the mine.

These profits built Capilla Guadalupe (Chapel) that stands today in the cemetery, the first church of major size in Catorce. The nine large murals that decorate the walls and ceiling there are a part of the original decorations, all financed by the "money bags."

Padre Flores was called affectionately "the man with the silver stomach" referring to the silver belt he liked to wear and the wealth which his mine earned for the church.

A lengthy report on the Catorce mines which was prepared by the San Luis Potosi Mining Association in 1851 tells of a second vein being found in the Padre Flores Mine in 1780 — a vein so rich that it brought the interest of Conde (Count) de Penasco.

MINA DE SAN AGUSTIN, PATIO INTERIOR. CATORCE. S.L.P.

San Augustin Mine was one richest

Mina de San Agustín, las más rica

MINA DE CANDELARIA Y FILOGOFAL

Clothing of miners indicates early era

El modo de vestir de los mineros — señalan la época primitiva.

89

"Suddenly, the Conde's men arrived and the papers showing Padre Flores' ownership could not be found," the historian wrote.

Then the Conde produced papers in his own favor and Padre Flores was "very annoyed." The good Padre finally succeeded in establishing his title and — the historian notes — even forgave the Count for his attempt to gain possession of the treasure.

One of the richest of all the mines was the Santa Ana, located at La Luz near the entrance to the Ogarrio Tunnel which connects Catorce with the outside world.

A mining survey showed that between the years of 1885 and 1905, the mine produced $25 million, most of it before 1900.

It was during those bonanza years that electricity was installed and President Porfirio Diaz came to dedicate the new equipment while being entertained on his historic visit to Catorce.

At its peak production period, Santa Ana Mine had not only a part interest in the tunnel and its electric tramway but had 25 kilometers (15 miles) of underground workings.

Santa Ana was the principal mine owned by the famous de la Maza family. In 1904, the company paid a dividend of 59 per cent on its capital stock.

Other principal mines included El Refugio, Guadalupita, Balenciana, Dolores, El Savacon, Descubadora, Alta Gracia, San Andres y Marona, Las Minas del Senor de la Humildad (the Mine of the Humble Man), San Miguel and Santa Genoveva.

As an example of the extent of the industry at its peak, there were 22 haciendas processing silver in smelters of rather primitive operations.

In addition to silver, other metals were brought out of the mines, including lead, copper and gold, in smaller amounts.

Purisima, one of the richest and oldest, is due for modern chapter

La Mina de la Purísima, una de la más antíguas y abundantes; está para cumplirse un capítulo moderno.

Ghostly Neighbors

Distinctive touches echo old Spanish influence in architecture
Algunos toques distintivos resuenan el influjo de la arquitectura Española

93

Lacy grills decorate old La Luz home
Enrejado de encaje adorna el viejo hogar de La Luz.

At the height of Real de Catorce's prosperity, the production was spread also to several other near-by cities and towns built on the same economy. These, too, have faded and dimmed with the closing of the mines. La Luz, Potrero, Las Catorce and Estacion Catorce do not have the rich history that adds to Real de Catorce's interest. With few exceptions, these had no signs of the luxurious life enjoyed by Real de Catorce's leading families. Even so, they still evoke the imagination as they stand today.

Potrero, first of the ghost towns after one leaves Cedral (and the end of the paved road), has a main street that is two miles long. There is a small nucleus of activity near the end of the street — a church, school and two grocery stores that seem to be the gathering place for the small population of about three hundred.

This town is about the same age as Real de Catorce. In the first decade of this century, it had a railway which connected with the branch from Cedral to Vanegas on the north. There was passenger service and a telegraph office. Many cars of rich ores moved through this station and a great deal of merchandise was brought in by rail, due for La Luz and Real de Catorce as well as the booming town of Potrero.

A few of the old homes were built of stone and even today show evidences of past splendors in their arched patios, carved stone cornices and heavy, hand-made doors.

La Luz was built around the headquarters of the Santa Ana Mine, one of the richest in the section. Substantial and beautiful homes were built for the owners, superintendents and engineers of the mine. Their families were with them and the social life was on a par with that of the upper class of Real de Catorce.

One particularly beautiful home was built by the Spanish owners of the Santa Ana, featuring a many-paned stained glass window in the drawing room and a semi-circular observatory, all built on a grand scale. On the exterior wall of the observatory, the family's coat of arms was reproduced and is still in good condition today.

This home, later used by the series of superintendents of the Santa Ana, also has a terraced garden on three levels behind and above the home. Retaining walls of stone, 15 to 20 feet high, divide the three levels. There is an elaborate irrigation system still in use, feeding water into the gardens from above the third terrace.

Two-mile long main street of Potrero is seen from road that climbs mountains above it

La calle principal de Potrero se divisa del camino que sube a la montaña visible en la fotografía.

Although unoccupied, homes along Potrero main street are well-preserved

Aunque desocupadas, las casas (en cada lado de la calle principal) están bien conservadas. ·

Each terrace was landscaped and planted with many exotic trees, shrubs and perennials.

Although the mine was closed in 1938 when the last superintendent moved away, this home and gardens are still fairly well-kept by the resident caretaker. Many of the plants still bloom and the fruit trees continue to bear.

A former superintendent recalls that the garden was reported to have cost two million pesos when it was first completed.

This is the home where President Porfirio Diaz was a guest during his three-day visit to the region in 1896.

Historians set a figure of 30,000 as the population of La Luz in its most productive mining era. Today, the count is less than 300.

Beyond Real de Catorce, still further west, are two more ghost towns whose past glories are evident amidst little present activity. Las Catorce, reached only by jeep trail from Real de Catorce, once had large haciendas where the owners' affluence was based on the mining industry. Here the altitude is much lower and the vegetation in the deep valleys is classed as semi-tropical. The fifty families who live here have year-round gardens irrigated by a bountiful supply of water flowing from mountain springs.

These families, too, have hopes of a new era when the mines will be re-opened.

Plans have been announced for a mine restoration project that would be headquartered at Las Catorce.

Further on along the jeep trail, one comes to Estacion (Station) Catorce, a village of 700 residents. Again the topography has changed and the village sits on a level tableland which is only about 5,500 feet above sea level. This town has an advantage over its neighbors since it is on the railroad. It has no highway connections, however, and is accessible only by jeep or rail.

Although Estacion Catorce is old, it is not deserted and has a modern outlook. It was established mainly as a rail outlet for Real de Catorce, its "parent" city, but the connecting road was never improved enough to move the ores in this direction from the mines.

Arched doorway of roofless house frames scene of past elegance

Este Arco, que es la entrada a una casa sin techo, sirve de marco a una escena de antaño

97

Entrance detail is "collector's item"

Los detalles en la entrada principal son objetos para colectores de articulos antiguos.

*Old hacienda included buildings, equipment for grading
ore before shipment*

Vieja hacienda incluye edificios, equipaje para clasificar el metal antes de embarcarse.

*Ore trains entered hacienda through this archway;
treasure hunter recently made big find on grounds here*

*Los trenes de carga entraban a la Hacienda por este Arco. Recientemente, los
que buscan tesoros se hallaron una riqueza allí.*

Las Catorce — series of arches once upheld aqueduct

Las Catorce . . . Una serie de arcos, en tiempos pasados eran el sostén de un acueducto.

Las Catorce was in its hey-day in this era

Las Catorce en todo su apogeo en esta era

OFICINA Y HOTEL DEL FERROCARRIL N.M
ESTACION CATORCE

Estacion Catorce's railroad office, station and hotel was center of activity (since destroyed by fire)

Oficina del ferrocarril de Estación Catorce. Antes que fueran destruídos por el fuego el hotel y la estación eran el centro de actividad

Station Catorce is "inland" town with railway its only connection with "outside" world; jeep trail leads to Real de Catorce

La estación del ferrocarril en Catorce está situada en el centro del pueblo . . . es la única comunicación con el mundo; la vereda de los "Jeeps" conduce a Real de Catorce.

La Luz (Refugio) Mine in full production (about 1910)

Mina la Luz (Refugio) en plena producción (Como en 1910)

Ruins of same area portray present status

Ruinas de esta misma area describen el presente estado

To collectors and serious scientists, career persons and hobbyists, Real de Catorce offers something for almost all special interests. It is a treasure trove for many such interests and an intriguing challenge for others who would do research in their particular fields.

Because of its topography — and of its very being based on the mining industry, Real de Catorce beckons geologists, rock hounds, gem and mineral collectors. Men of the mining industry are enthralled with the history of the early mines as well as fascinated by their present day status.

Old tailings in the mining areas as well as untouched terrain offer excitement for rock hounds, gem and mineral collectors.

History "buffs" will find treasure in the old archives of the churches and the Palacio Municipal and in interviewing the older citizens. Although a great deal has been written about Real de Catorce and its area in these old records, very little has been published. And almost nothing has been published in the English translation.

Architects find the old stone buildings fascinating from the standpoint of beauty as well as the method of building — many are tri-level — and the way they have weathered the centuries.

Artists and camera fans find an incentive in the buildings, the streets and the mountain backdrops and hasten to record these in their particular media.

Deserted old houses, whole streets of them, serve as lodestones for the artist's brush or the photographer's film.

Antique collectors are promised a field day here. Every occupied home is a potential "end of the rainbow" for those searching for old furniture, primitive paintings, china, brass and wrought iron pieces.

Those who collect the huge old wrought-iron keys will be delighted with the possibilities here. Each is hand-crafted and there are no two exactly alike or of the same size. All are over-sized to fit the thick old doors. Many are offered for sale with the old locks that they were made to fit. Collectors assemble the keys for display or use them as handles for antique cupboards. (They're handy as paper weights and recommended as protection on the water front — and always good as a conversation piece!)

Coin collectors will be interested here, whether or not they are fortunate enough to buy any rare pieces, because of the engaging history of the House of Money (Casa Maza), related in another chapter. Many residents collect coins as a hobby and for sale, especially since the collection of Mexican coins has become so popular among numismatists of the United States.

Heavy spurs, measuring more than six inches across, are Spanish heirlooms
Espuelas gruesas que miden mas de seis pulgadas de ancho, atavio español

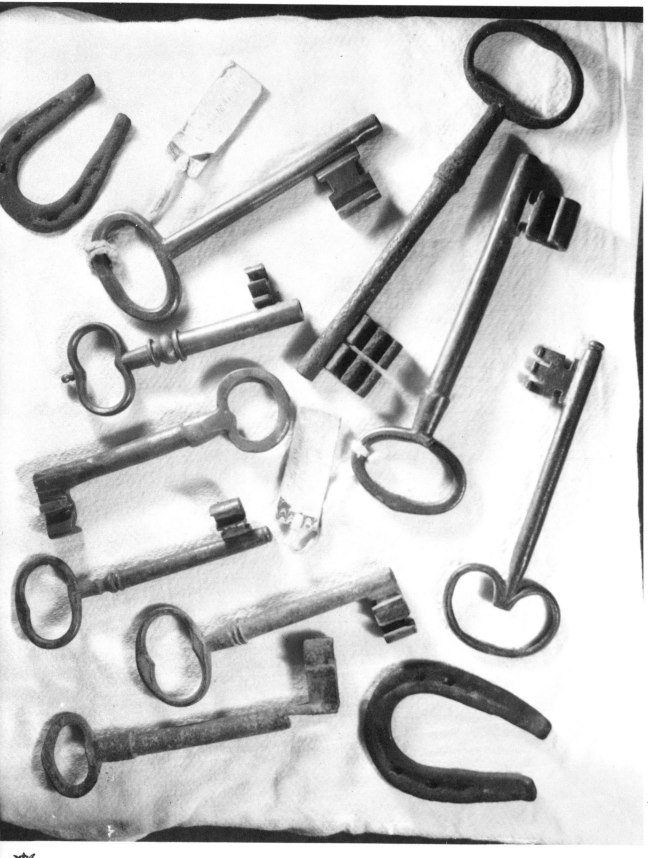

Keys opened locks in thick, hand-carved doors; small burros wore the miniature
"horse shoes"

Estas llaves abrían candados de puertas gruesas grabadas a mano
Burros chicos usaban herraduras miniaturas

Open fields of the whole section lure cactus collectors because of the many varieties here.

One in particular attracts collectors of an unusual order. This is the peyote (Lophophara Williamsii), considered sacred by certain Indian tribes. Those of the Huichol tribe of the State of Nayarit, send a chosen group each fall to Real de Catorce to bring back the sacred "button." The journey is made on foot, requiring 43 days, and is accompanied by many traditional ceremonies during that period. Offerings are made to the peyote and it is worshipped as a demi-god in their temples. It is said that when peyote is eaten, it allays both hunger and fatigue and that it produces multi-color visions.

Treasure hunters of another sort have recently harnessed modern inventions to use in still a different type of "pilgrimage" to Real de Catorce. These are using metal detectors to discover gold and silver coins, silver bars, antique jewelry and other articles hidden below the surface by early residents.

Since there were no banks, many of the pioneers used a corner of the garden for their own safety depository, especially when bandits were on the move in the region or when Revolutions brought changing times which called for extra precautions. Sometimes the owner had to flee to safer zones and many did not return to recover his buried treasure — or forgot where he had hidden it if he did return.

Today, some of the most exciting news passed around the neighborhood concerns such treasures that have been recovered.

Scientists with an urge for research in ethnology, economics and sociology will be captivated by the prospects for study here in a field practically untouched.

Because Real de Catorce was founded by the Spaniards in a region that had practically no native population, there is no Indian culture here as in the majority of places in Mexico where there is or has been a large population. Here one finds no background of Indian dress, crafts or customs such as one expects in other sections of the Republic of Mexico.

Couple this situation with the isolation which keeps Real de Catorce apart from the world even today and the results offer unlimited possibilities for stimulating studies in modern sociology, genetics, anthropology and genealogy.

And because of the unique history of Catroce — a "boom" town when the United States Declaration of Independence was being written, a near ghost town in the past half-century — the student of economics could write a learned treatise on this cycle.

Truly, here one finds something for everyone!

Along This Route—

Today's traveler to Real de Catorce follows the same paths beaten by the burros who carried out the great treasures of silver and gold during the 150 years that marked the town's Days of Glory. Along this same trail, the pilgrims coming each October 4 to pay homage to St. Francis must travel. (Many travel the distance on foot as a further mark of spiritual tribute.)

Some improvements have been made on the road and more are forecast. But most modern cars could not make the trip. Travelers are advised to hire a taxi or a pick-up truck at Matehuala for their visit to Real de Catorce. Some taxi owners in that city "specialize" in tours to Catorce.

From Matehuala, the road is paved to Cedral, an interesting old city itself. This is 12 miles from Matehuala, 18 away from the end-of-the-line Real de Catorce.

A log of the trip from Matehuala, in miles, shows:

	Miles
Leave Matehuala	0.0
Cross "Y" on Highway	1.2
Cross railroad spur	6.6
Enter Cedral	11.4
End of pavement	12.0
Old Grading Hacienda	24.6
Potrero	25.8
La Luz	27.6
Enter Tunnel	29.4
Leave Tunnel	30.6 . . . and enter Real de Catorce

Between Cedral and the old grading Hacienda, one sees very few signs of habitation. There are a few small ranchos, some with cultivated fields of nopal cacti. This plant yields the ixtle fiber used in making craft articles which form one of Matehuala's principal industries.

Many varieties of native cacti and a large number of native brush plants also thrive here.

Occasionally a large fox which the natives call Zoro will leap into view and scurry toward the low hills.

Goats are raised on the small ranches and invariably the traveler will meet at least one goat-herder and his flock along the road. The watering trough near the grading Hacienda is a favorite watering spot for the herds.

From a point near Potrero some sections of the road utilize an old railroad bed. This is the route of the rail line once used to haul ore from Potrero to the branch between Cedral and Vanegas. Old culverts installed for the railroad may be still in use under the vehicle road or may be seen as cutting through an embankment beside the road.

There is one other approach to Real de Catorce. The traveler may go by train to Station Catorce, a town of 700 population which has no highway connection with the outside world. From the station, a jeep trail leads eastward through Las Catorce and on into the original Catorce of the series, Real de Catorce.

This route covers about eight miles of steep trail, a scenic "tour" with its lush tropical growth in the valleys, and a winding narrow road etched against the rugged mountains.

However, very few jeeps are available for this approach and the traveler could not depend on securing one for his convenience, once he got off the train here.

(See the Chapter "Fragments of Yesterday" for a description of this approach, written in 1905. Today, the jeep would replace the horse or mule advised as transportation in the earlier account. But there would be very few other changes.)

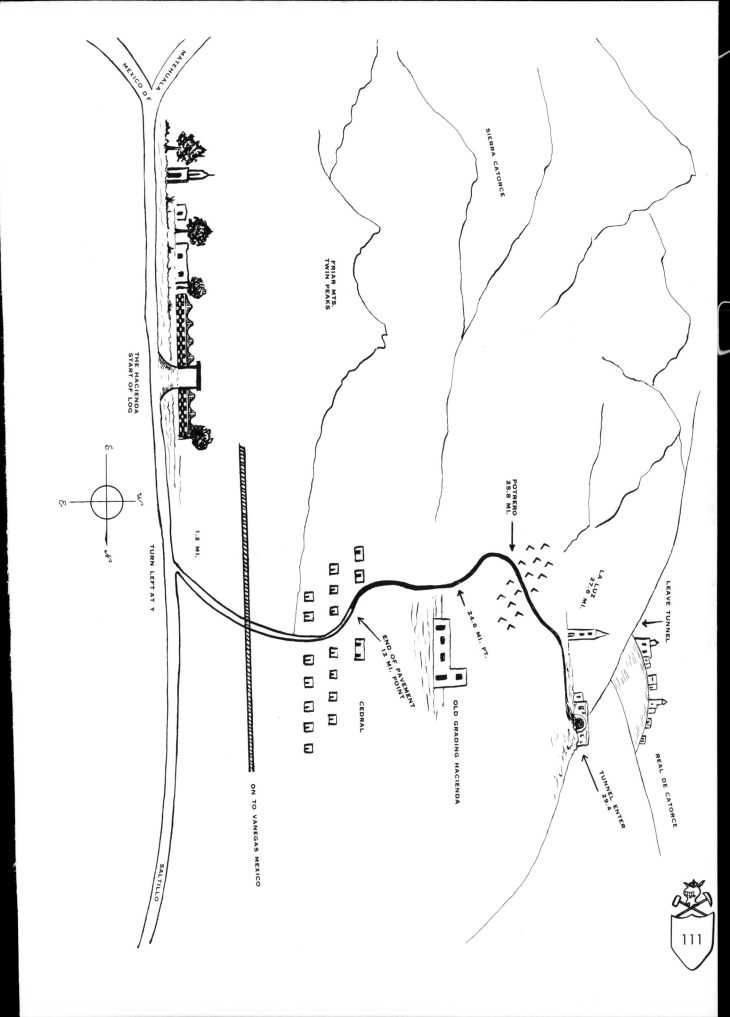

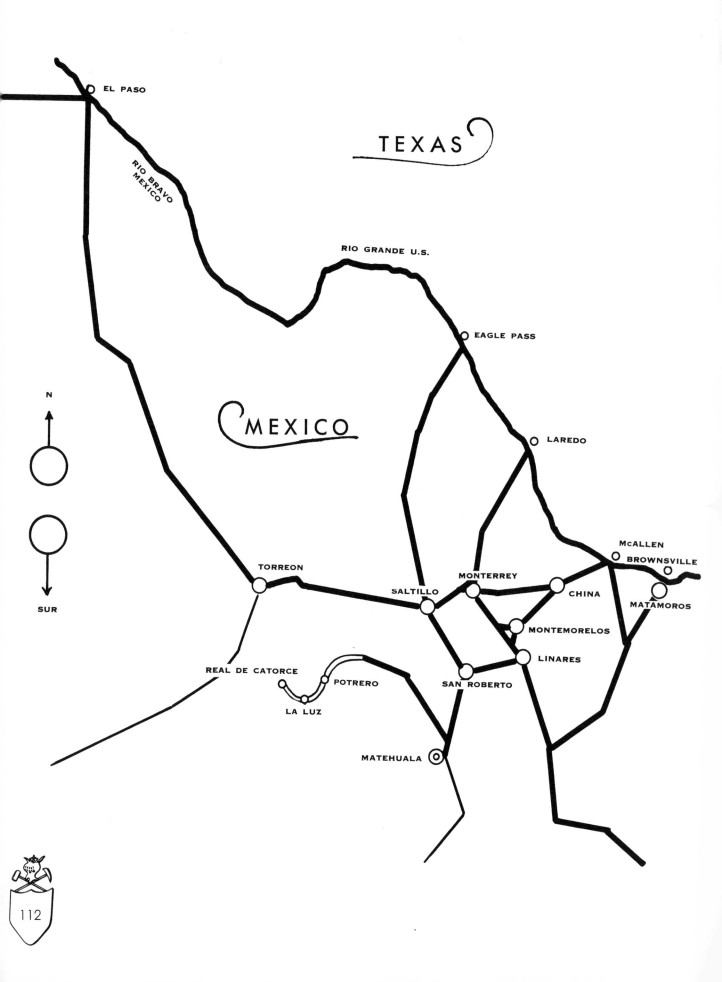

Fragments From Yesterday

Through translations of minutes of the City Council and other records on file at the Palacio Municipal (City Hall), one feels the pulse of history as it surged through Catorce — and left its indelible imprint there for today's visitor to see and feel:

April 13, 1796: Secretary of Tribunal de Mineria from Charcas to the Municipal Government of Catorce — It is necessary that there be land and springs on which the beasts that serve as machinery to carry lumber and other materials needed for mining be pastured. According to Article 83, Title 13th of our Rules, we ask you to notify us as soon as possible what lands and springs are available, whether they are public or private, their distance from the mines, expenses, etc.
Signed, Manuel Garcia de Ceballos.

✿　✿　✿　✿　✿

Copy of an interesting matter from the files of the Municipal Presidency of Catorce, written at Charcas about the mining discoveries before the office and authority were established at Real de Catorce — Juan Duran was commissioned to register or check the files at Charcas concerning land titles. He examined carefully these files dated 1770 to 1776 and some of later dates, only to be convinced that Charcas was not the place to look for the titles. He gave these reasons: On Aug. 11, 1777, we find the claim made by Sebastian Coronado on a mine on the Cerro (Hill) of San Jose de Catorce, opened up by Don Nicolas Barrios y Aranda, probably without registration and that he abandoned it. On Aug. 18, 1777, Sebastian Coronado sold one-half of the mine to Don Jose de la Pena from Saltillo, who came to live in Catorce. This mine was evidently the same one and it was named La Santisima Trinidad.

On Aug. 26, 1777, Coronado registered the mine "La Descubridora," donating one-half of it to Cristobal de Llanas.

✿　✿　✿　✿　✿

A dramatic break-through of Real de Catorce's isolation came in 1866 when a unit of the Revolutionary "Juaristas" captured the city. This story is told in copies of letters sent by the Mayor of Catorce to the head of the military unit at Matehuala. Catorce's government was aligned with the Maximilian rule and the Mayor's reference to "the enemy" means the Army led by forces on the side of Benito Juarez, now revered as one of Mexico's greatest Presidents and beloved as a leader of his people. The Mayor's two letters reporting the invasion of his city follow:

Aug. 22, 1866. Francisco Blanco Lavat directs the following to Senor Jefe de Politico at Matehuala — Mina de la Purisima Concepcion, de Catorce: The enemy arrived at the City today between 4 and 5 A.M., taking the guardsmen prisoners. They immediately gathered the merchants to take from them by force whatever they needed. They pursued the townspeople who tried to flee to the hills when they saw what was happening. The enemy fired on these and made prisoners of those they could capture.

I do not know if there are any dead or injured; as soon as I find out, I will let you know. One thing is certain, the enemy has left this town almost desolate, having taken so many people with them — not just the rich but the poor working class as well, mostly the latter. They have taken the store owners and their clerks. They have taken some of the most prominent people of the town.

I couldn't send word to you about all of this sooner because the enemy had us surrounded and no one could leave. Even I suffered bad treatment and I can only thank Providence for not being among the prisoners.

I conclude by telling you that I know not what to do. I implore you to name someone who is to deal with the government of this town for I cannot possibly continue as its mayor.

The enemy force is both Infantry and Cavalry, about 400 well-armed men under the command of Col. Pedro Martinez.

Signed, Francisco Blanco Lavat, Alcalde Municipal.

✻　✻　✻　✻　✻

Aug. 24, 1866. Francisco Blanco Lavat to Presidente (Jefe de Politico) at Matehuala: As I told you before, the enemy took all kinds of precautions upon entering our town so as not to be felt or noticed and not to let anyone out.

By 6 A.M., the town knew what was happening, especially after hearing the shots fired at people trying to escape to the hills. There they were met by the enemy.

By 7 A.M., they had succeeded in rounding up the administrators and watchmen. There was only one injured. They took $3,000 pesos worth of loot, probably more. They took men, horses, mules, weapons and machinery from La Casa de Moneda.

Of the important people they took, some have been returned after being treated badly. Almost none of the townspeople they took have been allowed to return. More than likely there were 500 men (enemy) instead of 400.

I will advise you on any other details as soon as I have them.

Signed, Francisco Blanco Lavat, Alcalde Municipal.

✻　✻　✻　✻　✻

From San Luis Potosi Mining Association records:
April 27, 1778. Don Francisco Javier Padillo and Don Ignacio Pruneda registered a virgin vein in the mineral of Los Catorce, naming it "El Patrocinio."

————

May 19, 1778. Don Francisco Javier and Don Nieves Martinez registered a new vein next to La Descubridora, naming it "San Francisco."

————

June 6, 1778. Don Jose Joaquin Mendoza registered a place on the glen of Los Alamos, calling it "Santa Eduwiges."

————

Oct. 1, 1778. Don Felipe Barrera registered the vein "Las Animas." On Pascual de los Reyes Feast Day, he registered a vein in Los Alamos, called "San Miguel."

Oct. 1, 1778. Don Felipe Barrera registered the vein "Las Animas." On Pascual de los Reyes Feast Day, he registered a vein in Los Alamos, called "San Miguel."

––––––––

Oct. 10, 1778. Don Miguel Caballos registered a vein on the mountains of Los Catorce, calling it "Nuestra Senora de la Soledad."

✿ ✿ ✿ ✿ ✿

Sept. 28, 1863. From Matehuala to Presidente de Catorce: The Secretary of the State Government tells me the following — The Governor of San Luis Potosi has instructed that outside of the Capital the circulation of the copper "cuartillo" (one-fourth of a quarter) coined in Casa de Moneda at Catorce is not permitted. He has asked me to inform you that you may immediately stop such circulation, imposing fines on those who do not comply with the new order. I feel sure your municipality could use the money (from the fines).

✿ ✿ ✿ ✿ ✿

Dec. 10, 1868. Three men were appointed to make an estimate of money (coins) in circulation at this time. These men feel honored to be appointed but they ask that their report be considered an estimate only for it would be difficult to give exact amounts. The request is signed by Vicente Irizar, Juan Mendizabl and Lazaro Echevarria.

✿ ✿ ✿ ✿ ✿

Dec. 21, 1868. Don Diego Gonzalo Lavin writes to the City Council and its Presidente at Catorce: Your letter of November 30 asks me to suspend the bull fights in the city. Contracts should be considered according to the existing laws of the time. . . . Six years ago, I was awarded a contract which states that I may conduct bull fights for 15 years. I believe I have the right to declare that I should be allowed to act according to such a contract.

✿ ✿ ✿ ✿ ✿

May 28, 1868. Copy of Decree No. 74 by Gov. Juan Bustamente of the State of San Luis Potosi: In order that the municipality of Catorce will be able to cover the deficit resulting from its expenses, 25 per cent of the taxes collected by the municipality may be kept there. Also, 25 per cent of the total may be kept for primary education.

✿ ✿ ✿ ✿ ✿

Author's Note:

Three bulletins on file at the Palacio Municipal and dated in 1870 reflect Catorce's part in the unrest that was being felt over Mexico at this time. Maximilian had been executed, the French troops had returned to their country and President Benito Juarez was seeking to unite his countrymen and establish a stable government. These three documents indicate the shifting loyalties of the people of Real de Catorce and of the civilian and military authorities over them:

Jan. 24, 1870. An official bulletin proclaims the San Luis Plan and pledges support. Signed by Jose Hipolito Sierra, Ciudadano General en Jefe de las Fuerzas de San Luis Potosi.

Telegram from Zacatecas to San Luis Potosi: Zacatecans will try to re-establish the Constitutional order of the Republic of Mexico which was interrupted Nov. 8, 1865.

From Juan N. Pimental, Colonel of the Cavalry, Political Chief of Catorce to his fellow citizens and compatriots: We must hold strong against the government of Benito Juarez. The dreams and hopes which Juarez promised us have failed to materialize. There has been no real protection for our people, only Dictatorship. We must follow el Plan Potosino, 1870. Signed — Colonel Juan M. Pimental.

⁌   ⁌   ⁌   ⁌   ⁌

. . . Real de Catorce, Circa 1905 . . .

A time capsule view of Real de Catorce is the gift of T. Phillip Terry whose *Terry's Guide to Mexico* has been the "bible" of all guide books, and whose first edition of this very complete book is a collector's item. In 1905, Mr. Terry approached the city by rail as his report below indicates:

REAL DE CATORCE . . . about 14 kilometers from the railway station, is poised on the slope of a precipitous mountain 9,043 feet above sea-level, in the center of one of the richest silver-producing regions of the world. It has a population which varies from about 6,000 when the mines are closed to 40,000 or more when they are being worked.

Travelers to Catorce can usually obtain a horse or mule from the railway station agent, or some friend of his. The journey can be facilitated by having the train conductor telegraph ahead to the agent asking for a horse and muleteer for the trip. The *mozo* who accompanies one to bring the animals back usually acts as guide. A horse for the trip can be had for $1.50 or $2.00 according to the demand. Time — about three hours. A walker with good lungs and sinewy legs can make the trip in about the same time, albeit the going is rather stiff and the steep trail is trying to one unaccustomed to cross-country tramping.

The foothills are visible from the station and the trail begins its sharp ascent directly from the edge of the plain.

No wheeled vehicle was ever seen in the narrow, precipitous streets of the town and good hotels are just as scarce. The only *meson* is that of Senor Rafael Salcido; rooms, $1.00. In the absence of lodgings at this place, one must apply to the manager of one of the mining companies or to some friend. Food must be sought at one of the *fondas* in the town.

A *Compania de Tranvias* operates tram cars (fare 10 centavos) between the lower edge of Catorce to the Santa Ana mine, passing the *Minas Dolores, Trompeta*. The region roundabout is fairly bursting with mineral wealth and there are many mines.

Catorce (Fourteen) derives its name from 14 infamous outlaws who once infested the region.